JUDO POEMS

Sid Kelly
8th Dan Judo 6th Dan Ju-Jitsu

Trafford
PUBLISHING

Order this book online at www.trafford.com/07-1864
or email orders@trafford.com

Most Trafford titles are also available at major online book retailers.

Designed by: Chris Robinson

Note for Librarians: A cataloguing record for this book is available from Library
and Archives Canada at www.collectionscanada.ca/amicus/index-e.html

Printed in Victoria, BC, Canada.

ISBN: 978-1-4251-4429-6

*We at Trafford believe that it is the responsibility of us all, as both individuals
and corporations, to make choices that are environmentally and socially sound.
You, in turn, are supporting this responsible conduct each time you purchase a
Trafford book, or make use of our publishing services. To find out how you are
helping, please visit www.trafford.com/responsiblepublishing.html*

*Our mission is to efficiently provide the world's finest, most comprehensive
book publishing service, enabling every author to experience success.
To find out how to publish your book, your way, and have it available
worldwide, visit us online at www.trafford.com/10510*

 www.trafford.com

North America & international
toll-free: 1 888 232 4444 (USA & Canada)
phone: 250 383 6864 ♦ fax: 250 383 6804 ♦ email: info@trafford.com

The United Kingdom & Europe
phone: +44 (0)1865 722 113 ♦ local rate: 0845 230 9601
facsimile: +44 (0)1865 722 868 ♦ email: info.uk@trafford.com

10 9 8 7 6 5 4 3

Table of Contents

THE TRILOGY

ACKNOWLEDGMENTS

When one considers what a small book this is, it is quite amazing the number of people who helped make the publishing of this book possible. To the following I give my thanks and appreciation for their willingness to give their time and talents.

To Mrs. Ellen Stevens whose computer skills made it possible to put my typed lines into the electronic hardware needed by the publishers. Truly, without this being done the book would just be in the form of Xerox hand outs.

To Mr. Terry Baxter whose eagle eye scanned and found grammatical errors that most people would overlook. Mr. Baxter resides in Beaconsfield, Bucks, England, with his wife June.

To Mrs. Glennis J. Orloff, Ph.D Chemistry, Princeton University, 2nd Dan Tang Soo Do, and Sankyu Judo (3rd degree brown belt), who helped me with some of the later poems. With her combined common sense, logic and knowledge, she pointed out ambiguities and possible misinterpretations.

To Mr. Chris Robinson, with his design of and suggestions for the front cover. Mr. Robinson is a judo student and local policeman, whose claim to fame is that of being employed as Stephan Segal's bodyguard whilst filming in Bridgeport Connecticut.

To Mr. Dennis Watson for his help and expertise regarding the Japanese terminology. Mr. Watson, a 3rd Dan in judo, is a former British international team member, who trained for three years at Tenri University, Japan. He presently teaches English and Japanese(language and culture) in France.

To Mr Jim Bregman for his fore-word to my book. Mr. Bregman won bronze medals at both the 1964 Olympics and the 1965 world championships. Truly one of Americas all time judo greats.

And finally to my wife and soul-mate Rita, who has learned to tolerate my mindless look. For untold hours she would try to make mental connection through verbal interaction while I was away somewhere out in la la land trying to bring the experiences, advantages and joys of judo into some sort of literal cohesiveness in the form of poetry.

Sid Kelly
July 2007
West Haven, CT USA

FORE-WORD

There are, alas, many judo teachers but there are few that have "walked the walk" of the full spectrum of judo and therefore speak with an eloquence grounded in experiencing the "soul" of the "art of judo." Mr. Sid Kelly is a masterful judo practitioner, a superb teacher, and a very rational thoughtful thinker. His insights and teachings communicated through the vehicle of poetry provide the reader with a wide range of in-depth observations which many would not see without him clearly and succinctly pointing them out.

Judo is many things to many people. All actions begin with a thought. You have to "visualize what is needed" in order to do it. To "do it" you have to "practice." To "practice" you have to "get up and get out." To "get up and get out," you have "to want the vision" you have thought. To "do it successfully," you have to "forget you are doing it" and "just do it." To "just do it," you have to have "practiced it" to the point of "living it." To "live it," is to fully grasp the benefits of the art of judo and its carry-over values to daily life and happiness. Simple? Not really! Practice, practice and practice sounds easy. Very few can actually do it. Thus, very few can actually understand and do judo. But if you do what is prescribed, you will always "get up one more time than you are thrown!" And it is in the getting up again and again that we live full lives and learn real lessons.

The Gentle Way has many lessons to teach if we are only receptive to learning them. These poems will provide thought-provoking ideas and observations which all should consider while proceeding down the long journey of "learning" and "understanding" the art of judo.

The more you read and the more you do, the clearer your knowledge of judo and life will be.

Thank you, Mr. Kelly for these insights into an art I love.

Jim Bregman
1964 Olympic Bronze Medalist
1965 World Bronze Medalist

PREFACE

It is said that everything begins with a thought. If you the reader are involved in judo in one way or another, you must have at one time internally suggested to yourself, perhaps I should try this judo stuff out: or if not exactly in those words, something like that. Then if you stayed in judo long enough for judo to affect your life, perhaps profoundly, as it has many others, it can be stated with a high degree of accuracy that that single thought made a huge difference to your life. However, before that huge difference could come about you had to experience the practice of judo, but before you could practice judo you firstly had to know what to do to practice judo. And for this you had to acquire some knowledge of judo.

Your judo knowledge was derived from two sources that can be categorized as either external or internal. External knowledge is the accumulation of experiences that previous generations have recorded and have passed along to succeeding generations. During the very early years of judo the learning of external knowledge was done by personal instruction. And still today, instruction from a teacher or coach is the most common method of receiving external instruction. But later, books became an added source of information from which the reader could receive information without ever having contact with that instructor. Today, with modern technology, external knowledge can be obtained from videos, CD'S, DVD'S and the Internet. As technology evolves, sources for obtaining external knowledge becomes more numerous and diverse. But this is not so for knowledge derived internally. For this, there is and always has been only one source: that derived at and concluded by the individual. External knowledge is first received and then processed internally by the individual. This information is then processed along with his or her other accumulated life's experiences and information. This old and new information is then interpreted by the individual and used in the physical world through the application of judo. In judo, as in any other athletic study, this is an ongoing never-ending process. It's information in, internal processing, and physical results out. In the physical world these external results are measured by their performance and refined by seeking more information to process. This process is the same for the beginner or the Olympic athlete. It's just that the accumulated knowledge and the intensity of application are different.

When a person begins judo the external information is quite overwhelming. There is so much information to learn. Learning how to coordinate the movements to execute, combine and counter all the throws takes years, besides all the holds, chokes and arm locks with their multitudinous applications. These two sources of learning, external and internal, can be subdivided into two groups: the first group brings about the skills required against a non-resisting partner (the conditions found during demonstration), and the second group is those skills required against a resisting partner (the conditions found during free practice and contest). The resultant learning in this second group is that of an internal instinctiveness, developed and derived from the inconsistent, non-cooperating conditions found during combat.

Because thoughts are powerful tools these judo poems can be of value to the enquiring, analytical, thoughtful judo player, coach or teacher. A new thought could change something in your judo, or set you off in a new direction of understanding. Poems are meant to succinctly express experiences, emotions and ideas and are written either in free verse or some form of rhyming meter. Ideally, the words, lines, and verses, and hence the whole poem itself, should be concentrated and free from superficiality.

These judo poems are known as didactic poems: poems that are intended to teach or instruct. All but two of the judo poems are didactic poems.

Poems are intended to be read in quiet moments for reflective meditative purposes. And hopefully, the reader somewhere, or perhaps in many places in the book, will ponder on some thought where a line or phrase will trigger a new direction of thinking, questioning or understanding.

The poems cover a wide range of judo topics intended to reach a diverse judo audience. Some examples are given below of verses from the book that are intended to inform, instruct, educate, elucidate, enlighten, be thought-provoking, and hopefully, entertaining.

Starting with the poem for the beginner, 'Hello to Judo' the beginner is given preparatory notice:

Most sports at first are easy to play,
Because one's motor skills show the way.
But beginning judo is a different story,
Because learning with patience comes before the glory.

Then there is the strong, super fit judo player who knows how to competently demonstrate a throw, but whose ability to apply the throw in randori does not match up to his or her demonstrating competence. He or she may benefit by considering the lines from the poem 'An Amazing Fact.'

So ponder on this amazing fact,
The actual act,
That creates the fall,
Is rarely taught at all!

Then there is the player who just wants to get out there and mix it up. He or she wants to have a good sweat and go home feeling great. In their opinion that's what it's all about. The thought of kata (pre-arranged moves) is just not for them. In fact they don't think it's real judo. Reflecting on the final verse from the poem 'Preparing and Polishing' kata, may or may not make a difference, depending upon the depth of entrenched prejudice.

If you find kata not your forte,
Let not your prejudices keep you at bay.
Improvement in judo is found by the seeker,
So look to kata to make your judo stronger, not weaker!

Then there is the fortunate player who has talent, but is unfortunate because he or she is too lazy to prepare and enter for a contest. The closing verse from the poem 'The Ultimate Test' (Contest), may do some jolting.

Some closing lines of advice,
For those with laziness as a vice.

Contest memories are the dearest,
And will remain your clearest and dearest.
So if and while, you are able and can,
Make contesting part of your life's plan!

Then there is the judoka who never leaves his or her own dojo. These judoka practice what is known as doorstep judo. These judoka never experience the teachings of other teachers or the diversity of randori skills resulting from the teachings of other teachers. They should ponder the message from the following verse.

Some judoka live lives of grand delusion,
Practicing in a dojo that's in seclusion.
Inside their dojo they stand tall, and never fall,
Outside they're small, and always fall.

And finally there is the old timer who keeps coming to work out but things are just not as they used to be. Something is just not quite right. Perhaps the two verses from the poem 'Playing Judo' (Randori) will put things in perspective.

The years gradually pass with randori the measure,
Losing speed, timing, strength and all you treasure.
So it's back down to the mat where you are able,
To holds, chokes, arm locks and all things stable.

Then when you're choked and groping for a trick,
And no longer quick, nothing seems to click.
Finally, when all is spent and you've had your fill,
You realize once and for all, you're over the hill!

If the following lines and rhymes,
cause you to admire,
They may inspire you to practice
and perspire!

HELLO TO JUDO

HELLO TO JUDO*

What's this judo stuff all about?
Will it increase my mental and physical clout?
After a lesson or two, will I stand tall,
Or will I just know how to fall?
These answers and more,
We'll give you from our judo store.

One hundred plus years ago in a land of the east,
A man had a vision from which the world would feast.
From an ancient barehanded method of protection,
He founded a sport and a system of education.
Using the hold and the throw,
He organized and named his system Judo.

The ju in judo means gentle, resilient, pliable,
But exactly which is not reliable.
The do in judo means the path or the way,
So the gentle way, is what we say.

Its growth was slow at first,
But as the acorn to the oak it did burst.
At first people's thoughts were utter nonsense,
As they believed it was just a system for self-defense.

Like all things do, through stages it went,
Until finally its message was sent.
Its message traveled the world far and wide,
Now it's one of the most popular sports played inside.

* A useful handout for beginners.

Then it was taken up by the majority,
As a sport with much popularity.
Finally it was seen with justification,
As a sport and system of education.

What's involved in this fighting art
That you are about to start?
The skills you will learn are dynamic and exciting,
Throwing, holding, arm-locking and choking.

Most sports at first are easy to play,
Because one's motor skills show the way.
But beginning judo is a different story,
Because learning with patience comes before glory.

When some skills are known the fun begins,
Regardless of losses or wins.
Applying skills in any order,
Brings to your partner complete disorder.

From throw to throw, or throw to hold,
Your attacks must be confident and bold.
If your throws or holds are not working,
Then you try arm locking or choking.

Physical benefits are many and varied,
And in your body they will be carried.
All is used from toes to hips,
Then up and out to the finger tips.

Mental benefits are many and varied,
And in your mind they will be carried.
Patience, alertness, concentration, are a few,
Through the practice of judo they will improve for you.

Sportsmanship and empathy develop,
As combat and friendship envelop.
Consideration and care for one's partner works well,
As successful results and bonding always tell.

Sport judo, challenging to play, and easy to explain,
Is to score a point, simple and plain.
So let's get to it right away,
Then your thoughts on it are for you to say.

THE GREAT HARNESS

THE GREAT HARNESS

You cannot change the laws of physics
But,
They can be controlled by the great harness.

Before you stands a mountain of a man,
Arrogant and threatening,
And seemingly immovable
But,
Ignorant to the ways of the great harness.

With explosive speed and control,
The correctly co-ordinated forces of,
Bracing, pivoting, blending,
Harmony, pulling, pushing,
Leveraging, turning, spinning, and gyration,
Are all unleashed with rapier precision.
He is unbalanced and overcome.

The mountain is unwillingly propelled,
Swiftly and effortlessly upward and over,
Following Nature's well trodden paths,
The circle and the ellipse.

Then downward,
Helpless and oblivious to his descent,
Assisted by Nature's force gravity,
The mountain's short journey,
Abruptly ends.

Shocked, shaken and bruised,
Prostrate, as a flat weathered pebble,
With ego humiliated in abject submission,
The mountain bears witness to,
The ways of the great harness,
Judo,
The gentle way.

THE CLEVER LEVER

THE CLEVER LEVER

A throw is a mechanical device,
Effective and efficient as a vice,
Whose operator is wondrously clever,
When following the ways of the lever.

This human clever lever,
Has to be focused and fit forever,
As applying a throw,
Is easily stopped in its flow.

From foot to head,
Judo skills are integrally fed.
With speed, coordination and timing,
The lever produces its rhyming.

All throws contain the inseparable three,
Kuzushi, Tsukuri and Kake.
Theorizing about them one by one is fun,
But often they're wrongly assumed to be one.

The Tsukuri and Kake are seen,
Kuzushi is not, because it's just been.
Effective Kuzushi is the key to success,
Without it, all is a mess!

Breaking balance is easy to discuss,
Even though it's the cause of much fuss.
Kuzushi is its Japanese name,
And has brought to some, honors and fame.

Slight at first, imperceptible to perceive,
Breaking balance begins to conceive.
Then stronger and stronger until complete,
Balance is broken and bodies meet.

Completing the throw, as if in a fast race,
The thrower's body is positioned in place.
Then after the action that's seen best,
Leveraging forces come to rest.

But the human clever lever must be more,
Attaining more by training until sore.
Training and learning when to pounce,
Requires giving it all, up till the last ounce.

Nature's mechanical forces are immutable,
With gravity as the example most suitable.
Natural laws applied to judo do exist,
And until Doomsday will persist.

Laws must be constant to be true,
So those applied to throwing are not new.
Here are some constants to read and ponder,
Even if not in awe and wonder.

The inseparable three, Kuzushi, Tsukuri and Kake,
Require time, patience and fortitude to see.
All throws contain a pivoting foot,
And success depends upon where it is put.
All throws contain a driving leg,
Exploding body power as a powder keg.
All throws contain an active leg,
Producing large actions, as hitting a peg.
All throws contain a power arm,
Producing upper power with devastating harm.

All throws contain a locking arm,
Securing the throw and causing alarm.
All throws contain an angle of attack,
Helping the thrown on to their back.
All throws contain follow through,
When completing the throw that's true.
All throws contain a determined spirit,
Otherwise the throw will have no merit.
All throws possess speed,
A constant friend indeed.
All throws contain synchronized timing,
Without it, the walls you will be climbing.
All throws contain coordination,
That's ultimately the cause of de-stabilization.

The workings of a throw can be a mystery,
Because what makes it work you can't see.
The eye only follows the Tsukuri and Kake,
And it's all over so quickly.

Kuzushi is leverage, the mystery unseen.
Understanding the mystery will make the throw clean.
Kuzushi levers are found to total five,
Bringing to the throw that sought-after drive.

Four types of levers are applied when standing,
Pulling, spinning, leaning and lifting.
The action of the fifth is rolling,
When the body is sacrificed for throwing.

The direction of the throw,
Is generated by the lever you know, or don't know.
The five levers are Nature's selection,
That govern all throws in any direction.

Whether the throw is to this side or that side,
Its leverage is as fixed as the tide.
For throwing skills to improve, flow and grow,
These immutable truths, you should intrinsically know.

The verses that follow,
Are lighthearted but not hollow.
Remember them if you can,
And perhaps you'll be your own best fan!

The Pulling Lever.
(Uchi-Mata)
Let the foot you place,
Leave enough space,
So uke can topple,
Before you apply full throttle!
or
TOPPLE BEFORE
FULL THROTTLE!

The Leaning Lever.
(O-Soto-Gari)
Let the foot you throw back,
Give an angle of attack,
That will produce a mean lean,
From which you can reap deep!
or
LEAN MEAN, REAP DEEP.

The Spinning Lever.
(O-Guruma)
Let the foot you place,
Leave enough spinning space,
So the torque you apply,
Propels uke to fly!

or

THE TORQUE YOU APPLY,
PROPELS UKE TO FLY!

The Lifting Lever.
(Okuri-Ashi-Harai)
Let the foot you plant,
Cause uke to slant,
So your upward lift,
Makes your throw swift.

or

PLANT, SLANT,
LIFT AND BE SWIFT!

The Rolling Lever.
(Tomoe-Nage)
Moving from your feet,
To your seat,
In a circular motion,
Uke's defense ends in commotion.

or

FEET TO SEAT,
USING
CIRCULAR MOTION
CAUSES COMMOTION!

AN AMAZING FACT

AN AMAZING FACT

Judo has been around for quite a while,
Although it's far from everyone's lifestyle.
Over one hundred years ago it came from the east,
Giving those that know a bountiful feast.

Slowly at first its message spread,
Some places it thrives, and others it's dead.
But spread it did, far and wide,
To countries with and without a tide.

Judo is now played by millions,
With judo lessons having reached the billions.
Technicalities have been considered from every side,
But the major one of all has been brushed aside.

The major one, concerns judo's major score,
The score that puts them on the floor.
The teachings of this major score,
Are concerned with closing, not opening the door.

For a door to be closed, like the end of a throw,
It first has to be opened, as you know.
The opening of a throw requires much skill,
The closing of it, next to nil.

So stop and ponder on this amazing fact,
The actual act,
That creates the fall,
Is rarely taught at all!

So what creates the fall, the actual act,
That requires such skill and tact?
It's breaking the balance of the opponent,
At any given or created moment.

This act passes unseen,
During entry, before what is seen.
When the balance is correctly broken,
It's as the correct word spoken.

Why is the omission of this important fact so,
On something every judoka wants to know?
Here are some reasons for you to ponder,
With perhaps a few more over yonder.

The first reason is found from judo's history,
Where repeatability is the same old story.
This is the way it's always been taught,
So no other way is seriously sought!

The second is you must find out for yourself,
Since this is true, it carries much clout.
Practice, practice, practice, has been the mantra for years,
Extending learning time by untold years and tears.

The third is, many people are quick,
To say theory in judo is too academic.
Many have no practical interest,
In mechanical theories they have to test.

The fourth is, throws were grouped into five,
Where teaching thoughts now strive and thrive.
The focus now is mainly on the end of a throw,
But without a beginning there can be no flow.

The fifth is, teaching something stable and seen,
Is much easier than what is fleeting and unseen.
The kake is visual, and can be taught when stable,
But kuzushi is unstable, often ending up a fable.

The sixth is, lever mechanisms are mostly unknown,
Pertaining to how a person is unbalanced and thrown.
All throws function around one of five levers,
And this holds true in all weathers.

The seventh is, a summation of the above,
New ideas are given the shove,
Avoided like the plague,
As they appear mysteriously vague.

So when you're on the mat, doing your best,
And failing to score with judo's greatest test,
Remember, the actual act that creates the fall,
You're probably not applying at all!

THE FOUR ELEMENTS
YARIKATA–KUZUSHI–TSUKURI–KAKE

THE FOUR ELEMENTS
YARIKATA–KUZUSHI–TSUKURI–KAKE

Traditionally, as we all know,
The elements of a throw,
Consist of the inseparable three,
The kuzushi, tsukuri and kake.

The kake is the throwing action,
Ending the throw after much interaction.
Tsukuri is the entry, which is easily seen,
Kuzushi is breaking the balance, making the throw clean.

The kake element was brought alive,
When throws were classified into five.
Since then most teachings tend to lean,
On making kake the central theme.

These classifications everyone knows,
As they are taught along with the throws.
They are hand, hip, foot, rear and side sacrifice,
That all fit into a package neatly and nice.

Classifications were made simple and logical,
As the classifiers focused on the practical.
If the hip is the determined emphasis,
Then this is where teachers focus their analysis.

Many think the kake is the cause of the throw.
But its flamboyant show does not make it so.
The kuzushi and tsukuri are quickly passed by,
To show what appears to make them fly.

Sometimes the teaching is to the extreme,
When the kake is the only theme,
Details on the end of a throw abound,
While what happens before is not to be found.

What about the neglected kuzushi and tsukuri?
From which a throw derives its fury.
The kuzushi and tsukuri, separately and combined,
Contain mechanical truths that need to be mined.

The kuzushi and tsukuri are integral when done,
But their analysis must be scrutinized, one by one.
The tsukuri, the entry, is there for all to see,
But the kuzushi must be dissected to a finer degree.

So what are these truths that when revealed,
Will give the finder results final and sealed?
Let's consider the entry, whose function is threefold,
As the following eight lines will attempt to unfold.

The first function is to reach the throwing position,
So the throw can be executed with precision.
The second function is to maximize power generated,
By movements fast, coordinated and integrated.

The third function is to opportune kuzushi application,
Giving a throw's success its explanation.
These three functions, when integrally supplied,
Increase the chances of a throw being applied.

If these three functions are to be realized,
The correct body position must be maximized.
If during entry the posture is weak,
The defending forces will feel and seek.

Using mechanics as the accepted law,
Leveraging is best done as if in a tug of war.
For optimum posture during an attack,
Shoulders should be forward and hips slightly back.

The tsukuri or entry of a throw,
Must never be slow.
It must be explosive, coordinated and timed,
Individually developed, after first being mimed.

The entry classifications for all throws number six.
With kuzushi and kake added for the final mix.
The six classifications are listed below,
With a line to help the memory flow.

Turning Backwards, is for the sweeping loin,
Which when done correctly they land on a coin.

Facing Forward, is for the major outer reaping,
With which the great Kimura sent them a-sleeping.

Turning Facing, is for the knee wheel,
Which when done correctly they hardly feel.

Sideways Forward, is for ko-uchi-maki-komi,
Guaranteeing an entry that is stormy.

Backwards and down, is for a stomach throw,
Guaranteeing that their bearings won't know.

Sideways and down, is for yoko-gake,
Guaranteeing to send them wacky.

Kuzushi, from the Japanese verb to crumble,
Breaks the balance, and causes more than a stumble.
By breaking balance and stability,
Throwing success increases in probability.

Kuzushi is correctly applied leveraging,
Which is the root cause of balance breaking.
The thrower's body becomes a clever lever,
Whose forces and fulcrum point cause the sever.

The lever is a simple machine,
Whose actions are efficient and clean,
Consisting of a body, a fulcrum, and a force,
Transforming human effort to that of a horse.

Leveraging classifications for all throws number five.
Which with tsukuri and kake keep the throw alive.
The five classifications are listed below,
With a line to help the memory flow.

The leaning lever, is for osoto,
That guarantees they go.

The pulling lever, is for the inner thigh,
That guarantees their journey is high.

The spinning lever, is for o-guruma,
Guaranteeing they go without a murmur.

The lifting lever, is for okuri-ashi-harai,
That guarantees they quickly fly.

The rolling lever, is for a sacrifice throw,
Guaranteeing the throw to be a fine show.

When all is said and done,
And the inseparable three have been won,
This alone is just not enough,
As more is needed when the going gets rough.

A fourth element exists, but never named in the past,
But its existence holds true and steadfast,
Verified by the traditional order, given without malice,
Go find the element, through practice! practice! practice!

Yarikata is the Japanese word for know-how,
Which when signaled, knows the time to attack is now.
This fourth element of know-how, is a sense and a feel,
Which is the beginning of making the throw real.

The three inseparable elements are physical,
But the fourth separate element is intuitional.
This element takes time and patience to possess,
With a history that shows a high rate of success.

Experience produces the know-how, the knowing,
Which prepares the inseparable three for throwing,
Who then apply their leveraging instinctively,
Producing the desired results most efficiently.

The know-how is applied first and fast,
With the inseparable three following last.
But learning the know-how has to come last,
Because the know-how just can't be learned fast.

A USEFUL JERK

A USEFUL JERK

Essential to a throw is the element of surprise,
When seeking the ultimate ippon prize.
As the beginning of the throw is the most tricky part,
What better place for a surprise, than at the start!

Throwing forces at the beginning are weak,
And defending forces will naturally seek.
So where the attack is weak and the defense is strong,
A surprise is needed to make the defense go wrong.

A useful method for creating a surprise,
To help gain the elusive ippon prize,
Is a distracting useful jerk,
Applied just before the throw does its work.

The verb to jerk, as defined in the dictionary,
Can be applied while moving or when stationary,
Is a short, sharp, sudden motion,
Assisting a throw with its sought-after promotion.

Although the action of a jerk is small,
It can add tremendous consequences in producing a fall.
Its surprise makes all the difference in the world,
As truth becomes apparent as a throw is unfurled.

Besides surprise, a jerk does more,
It's the crack that begins to open the door.
By applying a short, sharp, jerk,
Forces are set in motion that help the throw work.

The reason for applying a short, sharp, jerk,
Is it's a great assistance in making a throw work,
As it causes the defender to uncontrollably react,
Thus producing an attack that has more impact.

Using forces produced by the defending reaction,
Is a proven method that gives a throw added action.
By synchronizing with, and in the reacting direction,
Extra impetus is added to the throwing calculation.

During the first entry step a jerk is required,
Then what follows is usually admired.
The defender is misdirected on the direction of attack,
And because of discombobulation, ends up on his back.

As a guidance on how a jerk is best applied,
The following lines for you are supplied.
The jerking action is done by body and hand,
Then you play the music and follow the band.

If the throw is a right frontal throw,
This is the jerking action you should know.
A short, sharp, jerk to your right,
Will add to the throw that much needed might.

If a leaning lever is applied to a rear throw,
This is the jerking action you should know.
After a jerk to the front, initiating the attack,
The leaning lever will flatten his back.

If a lifting lever is applied to a throw,
This is the jerking action you should know.
A short, sharp, jerk, whose direction is downward,
Produces reaction forces that are needed upward.

If a spinning lever is applied to right frontal throw,
This is the jerking action you should know.
A short, sharp, jerk to your right,
Will add much to the defender's plight.

When a rolling lever is applied, as in a stomach throw,
This is the jerking action you should know.
A short, sharp, jerk to the defender's rear,
Will instill in the defender the desired reaction, fear.

So if you have a problem balance breaking,
Because your leveraging is just not taking,
Try a little something that may make it all work,
Begin your throw, with a short, sharp, crispy jerk!

JUDO'S METHOD
OF NATURAL SELECTION

JUDO'S METHOD
OF NATURAL SELECTION

Monkey talk involving natural selection,
Brings to many hypertension.
But this is stress that need not be,
As early man, irrefutably, did swing in a tree.

Natural selection dictates what is best,
Selecting the fittest for their final test.
Eons of time have proven this true,
Even when it was the opinion of a few.

Natural selection is not only organic death or life,
As man-made examples abound in daily strife.
The life of a film, a fad, or a popular song,
Evolves by the market signals of hello or so long.

Man-made creations come and go,
The unpopular fast, the popular slow.
This rule is governed without exception,
By the likes and dislikes of a population.

Judo is one of these man-made things,
Whose popularity once soared with wings.
Judo has evolved and is still evolving,
Through dedication and problem solving.

What exactly is it that people join judo for?
What do they expect from behind the dojo door?
People don't join judo to become a referee,
A coach or an official, even if it were for free.

Reasons vary far and wide,
And concluding which is best, should be put aside.
There's self-defense, fitness, sport and more,
But what they exactly want, you can't be sure.

After joining, do they get what they expect?
From judo's popularity, one can surely detect.
What is judo's method of natural selection?
What is its weakness that needs correction?

The judo activity, which is at its core,
Is what with a populous, must make a score.
Knowing that natural selection is the immutable law,
Let's carefully and candidly determine judo's flaw.

Let's follow the path of a judoka's life,
Experiencing the inevitable joys and strife.
Although this followed path is a generalization,
The exercise may bring about a realization.

The early break falls are tricky for some,
But by and large the job gets done.
Then when they've learned their first flip,
Their hooked into thinking judo is hip!

Then it's down to the mat,
Where they learn to hold someone flat,
With arm-locks and chokes they learn how to tap,
Stopping the pain and a possible nap.

So far so good, as everything works,
But this, with co-operating partners is one of the perks.
Time is now drawing close to seek the truth,
Which will require much athletic sleuth.

With mat skills it's usually a happy story,
As grappling skills have some success in randori.
Whether attacking or defending, prostate or prone,
They're asked to work within their comfort zone.

But the story is different in standing randori,
As evasive coordination is the required story.
Using free practice, their standing skills are now put to use,
Against resistance, with little sign of a truce.

Little seems to work, using what they've been taught,
As against stiff arms and a rigid defense, it all comes
to naught.
Then as they're battling away, doing their best,
They're dumped on their back, thus beginning their test.

Positive thinking keeps them from going home,
And the mouth chooses whether to smile or foam.
Judo, through the discipline of randori, begins to unfold,
As they're asked to do something without being told.

The difficulties that randori has now imposed,
Are far more stringent than they'd ever supposed.
At this stage many beginners reluctantly quit,
Even though judo had made quite a hit.

But when people quit they rarely complain,
And on the surface this seems rather insane.
But with randori deciding their way,
They become another statistic, by just fading away.

But for those starting judo at an early age,
The basics are ingrained, stage-by-stage.
Randori for such students is gradually learned,
And rough and tough randori is rarely spurned.

So these and some others do persist,
As judo's magic for them was not missed.
They doggedly battle on, determined not to fail,
But several years later their judo grows stale.

The brown belt ranks are judo's graveyard,
And it seems as easy to enter, as judo is hard.
So judo's free practice, its pleasure and treasure,
Turns out to be its selecting measure.

Although they have learnt many moves and tricks,
They find in free practice it rarely clicks.
Mainstream judo practice is rough and tough,
But besides the rough and tough, it needs some other stuff.

Learning this other stuff,
While engaging in the rough and tough,
Takes many dedicated years,
Meanwhile the graveyard is filling with untold tears.

The first stage of judo's natural selection,
Is selection by individual election.
Exit by the election of one, may not seem much at all,
But too many such elections, could be a club's downfall.

The second stage of judo's natural selection,
Is selection of a club's defection by election.
The defection of one club, may not seem much at all,
But too many such defections, could be an area's
downfall.

The third stage of judo's natural selection,
Is selection of an area's defection by election.
The defection of one area, may not seem much at all,
But too many such defections, could be a district's
downfall.

The fourth stage of judo's natural selection,
Is selection of a district's defection by election.
The defection of one district, may not seem much at all,
But too many such defections, could be a national
downfall.

The fifth and final stage of judo's natural selection,
Is selection of a nation's defection by election.
The defection of one nation is not small,
But too many such defections, could be the end of it all!

Perhaps an unhappy tale of natural selection,
With a tendency towards exaggeration.
Here, a case against hard un-monitored randori is be-
ing made,
Because, if this is all there is to judo, it will steadily fade.

Natural selection determines who will stay,
By rough and tough randori deciding the way.
If large numbers naturally selected are to cease,
Domination by strength, rank and age, must surely
decrease!

SOME ABC'S OF JUDO

SOME ABC'S TO HELP YOUR JUDO

A   Accuracy in movement, brings results to the moment.

B   Balance breaking guarantees they're yours for the taking.

C   Can't means you won't.

D   Discipline proceeds and procures the win.

E   Explosiveness you must possess for success.

F   Falling: As natural as a baby balling and crawling.

G   Giving in is not a sin, but it won't help you win.

H   Harmony is the flowing in the throwing.

I   Instruction: Inspiration or confusion?

J   Ju: Gentle, pliable and strong. It's hard to go wrong.

K   Kuzushi is leverage that produces throws above average.

L   Leverage should be all the rage, whatever the age.

M   Mixing dojos keeps you on your toes.

N   Narrow the mind and results are hard to find.

O   Overtrain and your enthusiasm will wane.

P   Patience in your practice will get you all you wish.

Q   Question all you're taught so your truth can be sought.

R   Read, read, read, read, read, read, and ideas will seed.

S   Speed is what all throws need.

T   Timing cannot be mastered by miming.

U   Ultimately, what you learn is determined by what you yearn.

V   Victory is to the strong and wild, not the meek and mild.

W Winning and losing: It's all amusing.

X Xenophobic attitudes produce judo platitudes.

Y Your kake will drive them wacky.

Z Zest in your judo is best. Lethargy is a pest.

THE REASONS WHY

THE REASONS WHY
REFLECTIONS BY A JAPANESE SENSEI ON HIS LIFE'S WORK

A question often asked,
For which to answer is a difficult task.
Why in the land of the free and the brave,
Is there so little judo for people to crave?

The answer to this is the same as,
Why in New Orleans is there Dixieland jazz?
It always lies in the history of the event,
So here we explain without circumvent.

Our story begins in a land of the east,
Where hard work, integrity and honor, are a feast.
The land is Japan where the island race,
Does everything at a fast pace.

For most of Japan's history it was closed to the west,
Without industry and technology and all that is best.
But Commodore Perry in 1854,
Came and opened up its reluctant door.

Forty years later they had their first war,
With their old foe Russia, they settled a score.
Gathering their forces of navy and marines,
They blew the Russian ships to smithereens.

Fifty years later, again at war, they did their best,
Challenging the mightiest land of the west.
Fighting with audacity and firm conviction,
Only to be overcome, by technology and attrition.

Fifty years later they're back on their feet,
Seeming as if, there had been no defeat.
With an economy second to none,
Japan had set an example, on how things are done.

Now, in Japan lived a man whose passion was judo,
It was said he was born in a bed in a dojo.
Here as a child he first learned the way,
Mastering the art, and practicing all day.

His practices were focused and fanatical,
Allowing no time for a Sabbatical.
From the age of seven, practice for him was heaven.
And as a teen, girls with him were never seen.

Then one day, he up and left the land of the way,
And sailed with his family far away.
To the shores of the USA he came,
To teach and enlighten was his aim.

With patience and skill the way would be shown,
Where the ways of the way were unknown.
The years passed by, and it was sad to say,
His hard work and dreams did not hold sway.

As an old man he could now accurately reflect,
All his shortcomings and things of neglect.
In chronological order his thoughts are revealed,
But because of pride, his lips are forever sealed.

From the beginning he tried his best,
 Working from morn till night, he worked without rest.
During practice his students he would hammer,
Stifling their protests to a stammer.

Then, with friends as close as family,
They organized and made judo history.
Each part of the country was sliced as a pie,
And each segment was named a Yudashakai.

Each piece of pie was headed by,
Friends from the internment camps, or the old country.
From the judo populace arose not a murmur or cry,
As concern for one's rank, was the key to security.

Using high standards as a front for control,
Rank was selected with a special role.
The first black belt was made nigh impossible to get,
Yet where judo was born, it was just the first step.

While the ranks of the plebeians were purposely held low,
Those of the high and mighty did consistently grow.
But the law of cause and effect remained supreme,
As Americans gathered in schism for their dream.

From all over the country the cry was the same,
Enough of this stupid duplicity, Shame! Shame! Shame!
Then another cry was heard: Let's organize today!
So came into being the USJA.

For judo to flourish and multiply,
New members must be in constant supply.
The solutions though obvious, were ignored
By the all-knowing Japanese board.

Back in the land of the birth of the way,
Judo is practiced far and wide each day.
Kano's legacy is there for all to witness,
To the schools, he brought judo and physical fitness.

Back in America, where judo was being ignored.
Kano's ideas were put away and stored.
With judo leaders lacking initiative, and all that is bold,
High school wrestling took a secure hold.

These mistakes, though bad enough,
Appear smooth to the one that's rough.
Difficult to detect, as it is most profound,
But the answer is seen, where judo is most sound.

In western countries where judo is well known,
Marketing judo, is its very backbone.
But in America, where judo is unknown,
Marketing is known, by its greetings of a groan.

Judo success is not found on the mat, as is supposed,
But how to the public, it is exposed.
Public acceptance is there to procure,
But only by methods that follow the culture.

Now he clearly saw his major flaw,
By keeping with the old ways, few came to the door.
But Dr Kano put the old ways to use,
By modifying ju-jitsu, he created a modern produce.

A smile now crossed his face, as a thought came in place,
Judo puritans and traditionalists would brace,
They would say Kano's protests would reverberate like
thunder,
This is a way of life, not some meaty hamburger.

True he thought, this is not a meaty hamburger,
But when it comes to marketing, he began to ponder,
Judo is only another product in this land of hype,
Where the challenge is to reach all, and every type.

The more he thought the clearer it became,
By using the old ways, things remained the same.
In a land of a quarter billion plus,
Marketing to the masses, would bring a surplus.

With his brain working at full speed,
He realized the necessary need,
He wanted a man, with or without a judo dan,
Expert in marketing, to reach every sports fan.

This approach is the American way,
Proven and tested and used every day.
Though not the Japanese method, for expanding the way,
It is the only way, in the USA, since culture holds sway.

This is the root reason why, he exclaimed!
And for all these years, the students I blamed.
The culture of one cannot be forced on another,
They have to work and blend together.

Judo was kept in an eastern straight jacket, he realized,
AND NEVER ALLOWED TO BECOME AMERICANIZED.
To teach and enlighten was his aim,
Using patience and skill, it had all been in vain.

The years with judo had caused him much stress,
He now had to admit, things were in a mess.
It was now time for conclusions,
Without any false illusions.

Here is the list that came to his head,
Although, he thought, they'll be here when I'm dead.

As always there were the exceptional few,
But by and large, the public had not a clue.

Judo in schools does not exist,
And because of ignorance, is not missed.

Judo has no heroes for the young to emulate,
This must be done before it's too late.

From judo there's no financial gain,
In America this is insane.

Marketing judo does not exist,
Therefore lack of growth, will always persist.

Then the very few who really care,
Are in different organizations, with communication rare.

Yes he mused: THESE ARE THE REASONS WHY!
Judo in the USA never got off the ground to fly.
This is the legacy we have of late,
If Dr, Kano were here, he would surely berate!

What of the future he finally asked?
To make judo popular, is surely an uphill task.
Each generation builds and learns from the past,
This is nature's way of making things last.
But one thing we pass on, for all to see,
Our old ways have failed miserably!

It is to new blood we now have to turn,
As each new generation has energy to burn.
Using modern technology, finance and new ideas,
Judo can become smiles, instead of tears.

By blending the cultures of east and west,
With the fighting sport that is truly best,
Judo, with all its benefits, will finally rest,
In the hearts and minds, of those so blest.

THE CLASS
THAT'S FOOLISH TO BY-PASS

THE CLASS
THAT'S FOOLISH TO BY-PASS

Connecticut must be every judoka's dream,
Or so it would seem,
Because you can attend a special class there,
That adds to one's judo plenty of flair!

The class is there for all to use,
But attendance shows many refuse.
Randori-ing judoka can attend this special class,
But most don't, because they just don't get off their —.

What word rhymes with class?
So to your head this message will pass.
Please help me here,
As this message must be made perfectly clear.

The idea of this special class is a gem,
Some would say it's the creme de la creme.
It offers you more than any dojo can,
Whether you're a beginner or a judo superman.

Whether you know it or not,
Whether your judo's cold or hot,
You have a judo problem that can't be solved,
Unless in your dojo large numbers are involved.

For your judo skills to grow and glow,
You need many partners to practice with and throw.
At the local dojo where there's usually four or five,
Judo skills cannot thrive, have drive, or be alive.

Some judoka live lives of grand delusion,
Practicing in a dojo that's in seclusion.
Inside their dojo they stand tall, and never fall.
Outside they're small, and always fall.

Attending other dojos will help your judo grow,
Ask your instructor, as he or she will know.
But if you're content with your judo class,
Then give this special class the by-pass.

But if you feel like venturing out a little bit,
For another judo experience in Connecticut,
There's a special pleasure awaiting you,
A class with partners far from few.

It's known as the First Friday Workout,
Which will give your judo that extra added clout!
No-one who attends will be cannon fodder,
As monitored supervision is of the first order.

If you have any unwanted fears,
You should know the class has existed for 14 years.
Every First Friday, judoka from Connecticut meet,
To play and test their skills and turn on the judo heat.

Experienced instructors supervise each class,
Making the First Friday class foolish to by-pass.
Each instructor has something unique to offer,
As they share their knowledge from their judo coffer.

Experiencing a variety of partners in each class,
Makes the First Friday class foolish to by-pass.
Randori there is supplied in plenty,
Whether you play hard or go gently.

The format is the same for each class,
Making the First Friday class foolish to by-pass.
Both standing and mat work are equally shared,
As with different partners you'll be paired.

Located in a brand new dojo, ten minutes from Route 8,
Is perhaps the reason why many are not late.
The class begins on time and never ends late,
Because after hours socializing is a permanent date.

So come and join this growing group.
Leave the comforts of your dinner with its soup.
Diversity of practice will see your skills a leaping,
As you follow the age-old law, of sowing and reaping!!!!

ANDREA LOVE
2002 JUNIOR WINNER

ANDREA LOVE
CONNECTICUT'S USJA 2002 JUNIOR WINNER

On this planet earth,
Many sports will test your worth.
One is sport-judo, where you must give it your all,
Before and after the fall.

And on this planet is the American continent,
Where few make a serious judo commitment.
But one who has is a girl named Andrea,
Who at sport-judo is an accomplished player.

From start to finish in a judo-match,
Her nimble feet make her hard to catch.
After keeping them at bay with her wily grips,
She then jumps in with one of her tricks.

Then over they go, more often than not,
Finishing them off like a fly with a swat.
Without a doubt when she wants to be,
She's a ferocious tigress for all to see.

Once a year the USJA selects its best,
But not by any dull paper test.
From each state instructors submit a name,
Of a student whose judo future may be fame.

Selecting a junior from Connecticut's best,
From the 2002 list was quite a test.
The winner had to be, beyond and above,
So of course, they chose Andrea Love.

With her good looks and charms, many do fall,
But her O-uchi-gari floors them all!
Where judo will take her none can tell,
So on her judo journey, we wish her well.

EVERYONE'S FRIEND

ELAINE MEYERS

EVERYONE'S FRIEND
ELAINE MEYERS

Cherished are the memories of the NJI,*
Whose closing brought many a sigh.
Memories range from those on the mat,
To having with staff members many a chat.

At the NJI the person Rita and I best remember,
Is Elaine Meyer, its most loyal member.
Many in the judo community may not know her name,
As hers is a mind with no claim to fame.

Through the years she was always there,
Teaching, organizing, encouraging or making up a pair.
Her love for the NJI and the USJA,*
Are such, that words cannot say.

Many hide behind a mask,
And talk and talk so people cannot ask.
But Elaine, with many admirers and beloved friends,
Has no mask, as she never waivers or bends.

All at Port Jarvis judo camp this year,
Heard of Elaine's troubles with a hidden tear,
However, we all agreed, those who know her best,
Her faith and spirit will rise and conquer any test.

We say, Rita and I, and all from the Port Jarvis camp,
She'll lick this problem like a stamp.
Our daily prayers and love for you Elaine,
Be assured, will never wane.

*NJI-National Judo Institute
*USJA- United States Judo Association

A MISSING PERSON

A MISSING PERSON

This year's YMCA camp was the best for years,
With plenty of smiles and few tears.
Spontaneous laughter filled the air,
And positive vibrations were everywhere.

But because of recuperating health,
My judo lacked its usual wealth.
Even the weak were too strong,
Resisting my throws that took too long.

Down on the mat the troubles were the same,
My holds were weak and tame.
My chokes did not inflame,
And my arm locks caused no pain.

Hard randori was not a consideration,
As it's now totally out of the question.
So there I was, on the mat, on my feet,
Transformed into a verbal athlete.

But in my spare time,
I would attempt to think thoughts sublime.
I kept thinking, there's something missing,
Like a man without a bait fishing.

I thought and thought,
But it all came to nought,
Then suddenly, it slowly dawned,
The more I thought, the more it formed.

Then I realized, it was about a missing person,
A person whose judo you could rely on.
Yes! It was Liliko*,
Because I needed someone I could throw!!!!

*Liliko Ogasawara. 4th Dan
Olympian and World Silver Medalist

THE TRILOGY

METHODS OF JUDO TRAINING
PREPARING AND POLISHING (KATA)
DEVELOPING JUDO (RANDORI)
THE ULTIMATE TEST (SHIAI)

PREPARING AND POLISHING
(FORM PRACTICE—KATA)

PREPARING AND POLISHING
(FORM PRACTICE–KATA)

The judo practice of form, which is to inform,
Is for many, the norm.
But practicing formal form, also to inform,
Is for very many, not the norm.

Practicing form with fittings or drills,
Brings either healthy results or unwanted ills.
Formal form, from Japanese tradition,
Is designed to enhance judo precision.

Kata, the Japanese word for form,
Elicits opinions that are far from uniform.
Some believe kata is the final word,
While others think it's madness, or absurd.

Competitive players prefer sweat and tears,
So they randori and contest away their years,
Leaving the moves that are slow and silent,
For those with less vigor and physical intent.

Kata enthusiasts prefer the meditative approach,
Although they too, are under the eye of a coach.
Moves are pre-arranged with less physical stress,
But much concentration is required, nevertheless.

If practicing kata improves one's judo,
What are the reasons that make this so?
The following verses reveal the reasons,
Why to practice kata through all your seasons.

Randori and contest are physically strenuous,
But kata offers a pace, refreshingly less.
Randori and contest make a player tougher,
But the finer points sometimes suffer.

Without fighting muscular constraint,
The picture of judo is easier to paint.
By studying one by one, judo's many parts,
One can overcome errors, and many false starts.

During kata study, elements are more easily analyzed,
Improving skills that can be practically utilized.
Fourteen elements are listed for you to consider,
Then you be the judge, does kata help or hinder?

BREATHING, exertion upon exhalation is the norm,
Exertion upon inhalation is inefficient and bad form.
The judo knack of, when and how, to exert and breathe,
Can be studied in kata, where one is less inclined to heave.

CO-ORDINATION, the multitudinous study of how.
If successfully applied, reaps the reward of a Wow!
When the mind and body coordinate as one,
The judo elements combine, and get things done.

DISTANCE, the space moved through to throw,
Allowing speed and power to easily flow.
Distance judgement comes with awareness and time,
So after a while, you can throw on a dime.

EXPLOSIVENESS, the rapidity of acceleration,
Will bring about the opponent's disintegration.
Rapid explosiveness means a greater force,
So in theory, you could throw a huge horse!

FALLING, to some the mere thought is appalling,
But in judo it's as natural as a baby crawling.
Falling here, there, and everywhere, without fear,
Is found in kata, with its lessons so dear and clear.

HARMONY, when two bodies synchronize as one,
Whatever the direction, the throw will be done.
Whether it's gyrating, rotating, spinning, or turning,
Harmony is the essence of flowing in throwing.

MOVEMENT, light and lively is a must,
Guaranteed to bring results you can trust.
Explosiveness, speed, and power, from it derive,
Results from which, are difficult to survive.

POSTURE, the thing that gets bent,
Because in randori, that's how it's frequently sent.
With an upright posture it's easier to attack,
So practice some kata, for an upright back.

POWER, defined as the rate of doing work,
And its consideration one should never shirk.
Body weight by distance moved in the shortest time,
Is certain to produce, results sublime.

SKILL, the measurement of how it all works.
And the finding out how sometimes hurts.
To make the elements all click, the years can be long,
So to help you along, look to kata's answering song.

SPEED, the rapidity of movement,
That supplies surprise, with power its supplement.
The greater the speed, the greater the surprise,
With the additional power, success is the prize.

TIMING, the meticulous study of when,
To pull or push, is it now or then?
Often, the only fact that gives an attempted throw its fate,
Is a matter of, was it applied, too early, or too late?

UNBALANCING, that tricky, tenuous, evasive, skill,
Which to learn, requires much patience and will.
But it's the starting point of the defender's end,
After unbalancing, the end is a rapid descend.

VARIETY, a quality so often overlooked,
When with your favorite techniques you are hooked.
With kata, your movements are forced to be diverse,
Putting static judo in the higher gear of reverse.

Truth, which seeking has cost many a life,
Is only accompanied with trouble and strife.
For judo truth, it is the test to be our best and never rest,
While seeking from form, free practice and contest,

Time wise, judo truth was established long ago,
By Judo's esteemed founder, Dr Jigaro Kano.
Eighty percent practice, five percent contest,
And fifteen percent form, he considered the best.

If you find kata not your forte,
Let not your prejudices keep you at bay.
Improvement in judo is found by the seeker,
So look to kata to make you stronger, not weaker!

DEVELOPING JUDO
(FREE PRACTICE—RANDORI)

DEVELOPING JUDO
(FREE PRACTICE-RANDORI)

Free practice known as randori,
Gives every judo skill a story.
Freedom of flow in body and mind,
Is the elusive ideal to find.

Randori is the soul of skill development,
With kata and shiai, a supplement.
To every judo player it is dear,
Undertaken seriously without fear.

For young and old, high grade and low,
It's education and experimentation, not a show.
Regular randori equates to gain,
Applied intermittently, progress is lame.

Benefits gained from randori range far and wide,
But only if pride has been told to hide.
After the ego is left at the door,
It matters not what the score.

But as long as the ego is dominant within,
Your only concern is to win.
Learning through playing is best,
So leave the fighting to win for contest.

Randori for you your problems will solve,
By and by your skills will evolve.
Movements should be light and lively,
Resulting in throws that are timely.

With body relaxed and posture upright,
Reactions will be right for the fight.
Trying often, left and right, front and back,
Increases the chance of a successful attack.

Randori can also be your enemy,
When applied incorrectly.
The object is for attacks to flow,
Then judo skills will evolve and grow.

But when arms are rigid and body is bent,
Being thrown is a rare event.
But then the object of randori is lost,
As it matters not if you are tossed.

The cycle of life is portrayed through randori,
Birth to death is an identical story.
When young the ground skills are favored,
Lacking speed and strength, standing is not savored.

When one is ready, the throwing skills are awaiting,
Correct moves are made without debating.
All seems to click, when you're in your prime,
As co-ordinated strength works every time.

The years gradually pass with randori the measure,
Losing speed, timing, strength and all you treasure.
So it's back down to the mat where you are able,
To holds, chokes, arm locks and all things stable.

Then, when you're choked, and groping for a trick,
And no longer quick, nothing seems to click.
Finally, when all is spent and you've had your fill,
You realize once and for all, you're over the hill!

To the young and able, of this advice beware,
At randori time make sure you're there.
Your time, so easy to misuse, but vital to use,
When missing a practice, only you lose.

Randori is your teacher, monitor and friend,
So regularly attend, so your body can move and blend.
Practice! practice! practice! while you can,
Otherwise, you'll just end up an old and desperate first dan.

ADDENDUM

Randori brings the physical and mental into one,
And keeping track of them ought to be fun.
What are your weak points? What are your strong?
Analyzing your randori will not see you wrong.
Here are some points, listed one by one.
All in all thirty-one.

1	Alertness:	On the mat you had better be, or the ceiling you will see.
2	Agility:	Movements nimbly or rapidly applied, which only the fit can provide.
3	Balance:	Stability and equilibrium is the game, with every moment being the same.
4	Breaking Balance:	Before the throw it is a must, otherwise, failure you can trust.
5	Concentration:	Attention to changing circumstances, will give you many advantages.
6	Co-ordination:	Physical actions in attune, giving mistakes no room.
7	Courage:	Having a brave heart, is a healthy start.
8	Decisiveness:	Conclusive, definite and without a doubt, will give your judo plenty of clout.
9	Discipline:	Bridge between thought and achievement, is a necessary supplement.
10	Endurance:	Bearing stoically all hardships, your confidence never slips.

11 Entry:	To the throw must be swift and accurate, or being countered is your fate.
12 Fighting Spirit:	The subconscious drive, that keeps your striving alive.
13 Flexibility:	Pliable and resilient as the willow, your opponent's only choice is to follow.
14 Focusing:	Concentrating on the exact moment, your skills you can implement.
15 Fun:	Enjoyment is recreation, through mental and physical relaxation.
16 Ju:	Being strong, gentle and pliable, your skills will be reliable.
17 Leverage:	One of Nature's laws, is, as always, without flaws.
18 Losing:	From your losses you will earn, valuable lessons while you learn.
19 Movement:	Unrestrictive, decisive and light, will always position you right.
20 Opportunities:	Are made, and come and go, make sure you're there, and not too slow.
21 Patience:	Is a classic virtue, as long as the results suit you.
22 Persistence:	When it's all over, be there, as the tortoise and the hare.
23 Posture:	Relaxed and upright, ready to defend and fight.
24 Power:	The product of speed and distance, applied correctly there's no resistance.

25 Reaction:	Against your opponent's attacks be sure, otherwise you'll be on the floor.
26 Skill:	That nebulous quality to perceive, only through practice will you achieve.
27 Speed:	The quantity of more not less, is essential for your success.
28 Strength:	When adroitly applied, to your skills it will provide.
29 Throwing Action:	The action between fit and fall, where you give it your all.
30 Timing:	When thoughts and actions synchronize, there's only success to realize.
31 Winning:	Whatever the outcome, you're a winner, when mentally and physically healthier.

JUDO'S ULTIMATE TEST
(CONTEST–SHIAI)

JUDO'S ULTIMATE TEST
(CONTEST SHIAI)

The paths of judo are varied and diverse,
But success demands you must immerse.
All roads lead to the ultimate goal,
Of making one's judo complete and whole.

Shiai, the Japanese word for contest,
Is the judo player's ultimate test,
As all experiences come to the fore,
When executing the decisive score.

When decisive scores are consistently made,
Hard work and training are being repaid.
Winning is the reward of dedication over time,
Resulting in satisfactions sublime.

Contest and practice are as night and day,
In contest you win or lose, in practice you play.
Contest is learning by winning and losing,
Practice is learning by your own choosing.

For contest proficiency there are no short cuts,
Many talk the ifs, the ands, and the buts.
Those that soliloquy, look to the outside,
But solutions are to be found, nearby inside.

When seeking, many factors come into play,
It's study and hard work, and some even pray.
But on the mat, in the real world of scoring,
You need much more to send them soaring.

One is that thing called skill,
Which to acquire is a battle all uphill.
The others are judo power and unpredictability,
Which when all combine, is a sight to see.

That evasive, slippery, shifty thing called skill,
Is a thing that you can never get more than your fill?
It's acquired only by trial and error,
And is known to be the cause of much terror.

Power, more tangible than skill to acquire,
Often becomes one's desire.
Power alone often holds sway,
But power and skill will have the last say.

Unpredictability is often beyond reach,
As natural talent is impossible to teach.
But as it's a quality to be highly sought,
There's no harm in giving it some thought.

High grade or low, novice or veteran,
You are advised to compete for you to get on.
For experience or promotion you venture forth,
Testing your mettle and your worth.

When entering an area to compete,
You often want to find that private seat.
With all your training, your stomach feels like jelly,
And you wish you were at home, watching the telly!

As fear is the only thing to fear,
Entering a contest can be severe.
But once begun, the dread quickly passes,
Justifying all your hard work and past classes.

To contest well, perfect condition is essential,
Rest and nutritious foods are beneficial,
Exercise and regular hard practice is the best,
If one is to meet the ultimate test.

To be fully prepared for contest,
Relying only on physical prowess is not best.
One needs an overall strategy to win,
With some tactics to see you through thick and thin.

Sometimes it seems, all is not at your door,
When referee, judges, and opponent, all four,
Are doing more and more and more,
To keep you from your well earned score.

So learn the contest rules with glee,
To help your matches stay penalty free.
Time spent off the mat in this endeavor,
Will on the mat reward you forever.

When young and in the prime of life,
The desire to contest is strong and rife.
This is the time to practice hard and long,
To be prepared and forever strong.

If your training is sincerely done,
Then even if you lose, you will have won.
Sincere training shows up on the mat,
When all your opponents' backs become flat.

Your ego can be friend or foe,
And how to handle it you must know.
If your ego is not left at the door,
More often than not, you'll see the floor.

Ego as a friend will give you drive,
And keep your determination alive.
But as a foe, it may say no,
When your ippons cease to show.

Some closing lines of advice,
For those with laziness as a vice.

Contest memories are the dearest,
And will remain your clearest and nearest,
So if, and while, you are able and can,
Make contesting part of your life plan.

UNDERSTANDING JUDO

UNDERSTANDING JUDO

YOU SEE.
YOU TRY.
YOU FAIL.

IT IS EXPLAINED,
YOU TRY.
YOU FAIL.

IT IS EXPLAINED AGAIN.
YOU TRY.
YOU TRY.
YOU FAIL.

YOU THINK ABOUT IT.
YOU TRY.
YOU TRY.
YOU TRY.
YOU FAIL.

YOU THINK ABOUT IT,
AGAIN AND AGAIN.
YOU TRY.
YOU TRAIN.
YOU FAIL.

YOU KEEP THINKING ABOUT IT.
YOU VISUALIZE ABOUT IT.
YOU TRY.
YOU TRAIN.
YOU TRAIN.
YOU FAIL.

YOU READ ABOUT IT.
YOU KEEP THINKING ABOUT IT.
YOU KEEP VISUALIZING ABOUT IT..
YOU TRAIN.
YOU TRAIN.
YOU TRAIN.
YOU FAIL.
OTHERS GIVE UP.

YOU WATCH VIDEOS ON IT.
YOU KEEP READING ABOUT IT.
YOU KEEP THINKING ABOUT IT.
YOU KEEP VISUALIZING ABOUT IT..
YOU TRAIN.
YOU TRAIN.
YOU TRAIN.
YOU TRAIN.
YOU FAIL.
MORE GIVE UP.

YOU WATCH MORE VIDEOS ON IT.
YOU KEEP READING ABOUT IT.
YOU KEEP THINKING ABOUT IT.
YOU KEEP VISUALIZING ABOUT IT.
YOU TRAIN.
YOU TRAIN.
YOU TRAIN.
YOU TRAIN.
YOU TRAIN.
YOU TRAIN.
YOU TRAIN.
YOU TRAIN.
AND

SOMETIMES

YOU SUCCEED!

PLEASE ANSWER THE QUESTION ON THE NEXT PAGE.

DO YOU UNDERSTAND?

JAPANESE TERMINOLOGY
USED IN THE POEMS

In consideration of the people who are not acquainted with judo and its terminology, the use of Japanese words in the poems was kept at a minimum. However, some were used and some just had to be used. For the interested reader these words are explained below.

Dojo	Exercise hall for the practice of martial arts.
Dr Kano	Founder of Kodokan judo, officially formed in 1882.
Judo	A sport and system of education to train the mind and body. Ju(gentle), do(the way). The gentle way.
Judoka	A practitioner of judo. Formerly, a judo expert.
Ju-jitsu	A system of self-defense from which judo was derived.
Kake	The throwing action. The action executed at the latter part of a throw after the balance of the opponent has been successfully broken and the entry completed.
Kata	Form practice. The practice of pre-arranged moves against a non-resisting partner.
Ko-uchi maki-komi	Minor inner winding throw.
Kuzushi	Breaking the balance of the opponent during the entry of a throw. From the verb to crumble.

O-guruma	Major wheel throw.
O-kuri ashi-harai	Sweeping ankle throw.
O-soto-gari	Major outer reaping throw.
O-uchi-gari	Major inner reaping throw.
Randori	Free exercise. A method of training to develop the judo skills of throwing, holding, choking and arm locking against a resisting partner.
Sensei	Teacher. Literally, one who has been before.
Shiai	Contest. The testing of one's judo skills against other judoka.
Tomoe-nage	Circle throw. Usually known as stomach throw.
Tsukuri	The entry of a throw during which the balance-breaking action is applied.
Uchi-mata	Inner thigh throw.
Yarikata	Know how: Feel and intuition derived from practical experience.
Yoko-gake	Side dash throw.
Yudanshakai	Association of black belt holders. Name given to an area judo organization, e.g, The New York Yadanshakai.

ABOUT THE AUTHOR

Sid Kelly began judo in 1957 in London, England, under the tutelage of the renowned technician and pre-second world war judo champion, Kenshiro Abe. He then trained for four years at the Renshudan JC under the guidance of Mr. Leggett, Mr. G Kerr and Mr. J. Newman. In 1960 he won the British Judo Council (BJC) black belt championships and during 1965/6/7 he represented Gt Britain with the British Judo Association (BJA) on nine occasions in international matches. He was the head instructor at the Renrukan Judo Club, Uxbridge, Middx (1960-1967) where three of its members were in the British judo team. He passed the Coach Award Examination, was Assistant Area Coach for the NHC (Northern Home Counties), captained the NHC team that won the Area Championships in 1966, and won Britain's first Kata competition in the NHC Area Championships.

Emigrated to the USA in 1967. Was overall winner of the New England Black Belt Championships, Connecticut State Champion, ten years National Referee, two times gold medalist in the Worlds Masters (Canada 1999),(Japan 2004), coach of the winning Connecticut team (1999 United States Judo Association(USJA) National team Championships), USJA Certified Coach, Master Examiner and Kata Examiner. In Connecticut, introduced grass roots programs for: Junior and Senior Leagues, the first Friday of the month work outs, Senior Club Visits, Junior training sessions, Kata sessions for Connecticut instructors and monthly visits by out-of-state instructors.

Sid Kelly has written two books, Lesson Plans and Combat Games and produced eight videos in two sets – five on "Preparing for your Judo Promotion", and three on "A Definitive Study of Wake-Gamatme – 70 applications". He has also developed and documented the following Sequence Judo Training Drills:

a) Standing sequences . b) Ashi-Waza. c) Throws to Holds. d)

Holds and escapes. e) Groundwork Escapes-Counters. f) Throws to Strangles. g) Strangles. h) Throws to Arm Locks. j) Arm Lock. k) Juji-Gatame. l) Ude-Garame. m) Kata-Juji-Jime. n) Standing Arm Locks. o) Mirror Imaging (a method to improve forms of falling). p) Cardio Judo (aerobic exercises for the non-judoka using movements found specifically in judo).

He holds the rank of 8th Dan Judo, 6th Dan Ju-jitsu.

He is a qualified engineer with a Higher National Diploma in Mechanical Engineering (with 2 distinctions) and is now retired after working 47 years as a mechanical designer in the field of high speed automation equipment.

He lives with his wife Rita, in West Haven, Connecticut, USA and has two children, Susan and Tom, and three grandsons, Beau, Atticus and Thaddeus.

In his retirement, Sid Kelly teaches judo and conducts clinics. Besides the usual teaching of throws, holds, arm locks, chokes, turn overs, etc., Sid Kelly's clinics emphasize and specialize in skill training drills and the now largely ignored subject of fundamental principals. Clinic enquiries can be made by contacting: skelly111@comcast.net

ISBN 142514429-2

9 781425 144296